Who will cry for the little boy
- Antwone Fischer

"Who will cry for the little boy,
Lost and all alone?
Who will cry for the little boy,
Abandoned without his own?
Who will cry for the little boy?
He cried himself to sleep.
Who will cry for the little boy?
He never had for keeps.
Who will cry for the little boy?
He walked the burning sand.
Who will cry for the little boy?
The boy inside the man.
Who will cry for the little boy?
Who knows well hurt and pain.
Who will cry for the little boy?
He died and died again.
Who will cry for the little boy?
A good boy he tried to be.
Who will cry for the little boy,
Who cries inside of me?"

HOW TO RAISE A MAN ... Not A Momma's Boy!

Glenn P. Brooks, Jr.
(A Recovering Momma's Boy)

HOW TO RAISE A MAN…
NOT A MOMMA'S BOY!

2nd Edition.

Copyright © 2012

Glenn P. Brooks, Jr.

Cover Design by Vexed Graphics

For more information visit us online at
www.mommasboy.org
www.constantrelationshipcoaching.com

For more information regarding workshops and speaking engagements
thecrcoach@gmail.com

DEDICATION

This book is dedicated to my mom and all women who are faced with the challenge of having to raise a boy.

My prayer is that God would give you strength, courage, and favor as you stay the course.
Your son needs the healthy you.

Table of Contents

INTRODUCTION

When I was first inspired to write this book I had no clue on how many lives it would touch. I'm so glad that I allowed myself to be challenged by a very dear friend to put pen to paper and release the first edition. Since the initial release I have been completely humbled by the comments from so many mothers who couldn't say thank you enough to me for providing them with an inside view on how boys think and respond to being raised without a father. Through my personal experience and the experiences of others I have been able to expose many of the pitfalls that mothers fall into when raising their sons alone.

I never would have imagined that men would comment on the book they way they have. From them being able to identify with the material personally to being able to recognize why their sons are the way they are. Men have been able to admit that even though they may be in the home, their lack of involvement in the lives of their sons has produced a "Momma's Boy". This is not a book just for mothers but for all parents of sons.

In response to the many comments I've received I am releasing the 2nd edition of "How To Raise A Man... Not A Momma's Boy" which highlights some of the key points that when embraced and applied will help you to raise your son successfully. My hope is that you do more than read this book, but apply it.

This book is for parents whose goal is to better understand their sons and do their best to raise their sons to become healthy men.

ONE
Momma's Boy Under Construction

I still remember standing in the doorway of the bathroom, staring up at this big man. Looking back on it, he wasn't exceptionally tall. But to me, he was the tallest, strongest man in the world. I still remember him examining his chin in the mirror, finishing that manly ritual that was so fascinating to me as a four-year-old. "Daddy, what are you doing?" I asked him, even though I knew. I just wanted to talk to him. "Shaving, son." I can still hear his voice. "Can I shave?" my little voice pleaded. "You're not old enough, son. Once you get older, you can shave"

I think all little boys long for their fathers to teach them boy stuff that later shapes their manhood, basic stuff like riding a bike, playing football, learning to defend themselves, and even how to shave. Activities help to shape a boys mind, teaching him discipline, patience, attention to detail and persistence. This ultimately helps to develop character. However, for me those lessons wouldn't come for a long time and would not come from my natural father.

Back in the day, my dad was a drill sergeant at Ft. Jackson, South Carolina. My parents were still together then, but I remember that my father was rarely home. But he was my dad. His face and his image were burned into my heart, even though he hardly ever did much for me, or spent much time with me. Still, he was my dad.

Then all too suddenly, before I was even old enough to know what was happening, it was over. The beginning of the end began with a long train-ride from South Carolina back to Maryland. I knew it was a train because it rattled and shook all night. I floated in and out of sleep for hours. I kept peering out the window expecting to see daylight, but all I saw was black. I kept wondering, "Why can't I see out the window?" Everything was so confusing and so dark! "Go back to sleep son, it's still dark", my mother said in the most reassuring voice. I can still feel the comfort she gave me in those few words. My mother's voice was the only voice I heard and would hear for quite some time, because my dad would no longer be that essential part of my life.

I didn't realize it then, but my parents were getting divorced. It wouldn't be final for another two years, but that hardly mattered. My father was gone. It was just my mom, my little sister, and me. For years, my sister and I would ask for him. "When is Daddy coming home?" "Will he be here tomorrow?" My sister and I still shared a room back then and I can remember us whispering together after we were supposed to be asleep. We imagined what it would be like once Daddy came back, and we were a family again. Even as crazy as my childhood was, it was the only "normal" I knew.

I've been through a lot and I'm sure you have too, but it's hard for me to think of anything more painful than the gaping wound in the heart of child aching for his father. I knew I wanted my father back, yet there was no way I could've realized back then how much his absence would change my life forever. I'm not talking about a bunch of talk-show drama like, "I hate my dad, and that's why I'm messed up." It's the easiest thing in the world to blame everything on our parents. No, I'm talking about my emotional, mental, and spiritual development-how that ultimately altered the course of my life because my father was missing in action.

Ugly Reality

I was probably eight years old by the time I finally accepted that he wasn't coming home. I remember overhearing that he had remarried and soon after that, my mom started dating. The fact that my mom never explained to me what was going on was one of her first big mistakes. My mom wasn't a terrible person and like a lot of women in her situation she just did what came naturally, which was to hug me and hold me, because my mother was very affectionate and that was often the only comfort I knew.

HERE'S A THOUGHT:
Children crave balance, they need both affection and boundaries. All of one or the other disrupts their world.

Today I understand that when I was a kid back in the early seventies, parents weren't taught or expected to do a whole lot of explaining. But, there was lots of wisdom in "Old School" parenting that made a lot of sense, sense that parents today would do well to remember. There was the wisdom of working hard, providing for your family and disciplining your children. But at the same time, a parent had to be willing to provide their children with responsible answers to their questions. Maybe I wouldn't have understood everything at four years old, even if my mom had told me everything. But in my opinion, it's part of a parent's responsibility to help their children process life-experiences, especially the traumatic events of their young lives. Even burdened single mothers, going through the most difficult times in their lives must find a way to tell their kids what's happening, in terms they can understand.

Sure, it's hard to explain to a four or five-year-old what divorce means. Sure, it's painful for you to see that "look" in his eyes. Of course, it's much easier to ignore the situation, to tell yourself he's too young to understand and force him to figure it out on his own. It's at this point that you may consider talking with a professional counselor or someone who's been formally trained in how to handle family issues. If your son is going through something as traumatic as "Divorce" and you choose not to get him some serious help to process his thoughts, what you're really telling him, without saying a word, is that he can't look to you for guidance and wisdom and understanding. If he can only come to you for hugs and goodies, you're setting him on a course to become a Momma's Boy.

My definition of a Momma's Boy is a male who thinks, responds, and in some cases behaves (emotionally) like a female. When the mother who is parenting alone settles for providing temporary, inadequate relief to her son's emotional pain, she has lost sight of the goal of raising her son to be the man he's supposed to be. This sets a pattern for boys to view women as vehicles to calm their urges, not individuals to be respected. I know, because that's exactly what happened to me.

Missing in Action

I remember growing up and only spending time with my dad, on average, maybe once or twice a year. Basically, my dad would come through once a year to spend quality time with me and my sister. We would go out for the day or stay at his house for the weekend. I remember one time my father had promised to pick us up. My sister and I both got dressed and patiently waited. Periodically, throughout that day he would call to assure us he was on his way. First, he promised he would be there in an hour. Then, two hours later it was, "I'll be there in twenty minutes".

The minutes soon turned into hours and before long, the entire day was gone. We didn't even eat because we just knew he was coming at any moment; finally the phone calls stopped and Daddy never did show up. To this day when I think about it I can still feel the pain of that little boy and his sister in the window waiting for our father.

Like so many other boys in my situation, I learned early not to trust men. I also learned a ferocious dependence on women, which would later rage against any efforts I made to provide for or protect the women in my life. I became the worst kind of dog; the kind that everybody likes at first; you know the kind - nice personality, intelligent, nice looking, good job, and somebody that you could really see yourself with. Then it would happen. I'd bite you and rip your heart out because by now I'm bored and thinking about other options. By now, I'd be off actively thinking about life with someone else. I was the most self-absorbed dude you could imagine meeting. Unfortunately it wasn't until you were badly bitten that you would find that out. By that time, the damage was done and I'd selfishly move on. I had turned out just like my father and I hated it! Although my mother made her share of mistakes as well, she never deserted me; she was always there. Even in the times when she had to work several jobs, whenever she promised something, she delivered.

Growing up as the only boy with no father took its toll, especially when it came to defending myself. We all know that kids can be cruel. That's a fact of life. But just like girls need a mom to talk about the jealousy and gossip they have to deal with, boys also desperately need a father to talk to about the bullies, the harassment and "the playground" in general. It's easy as an adult to look at that stuff and think, "He'll live through it-everyone goes through that." But, for the boy who's living through this misery, it doesn't feel like everything's going to be okay.

HERE'S A THOUGHT:

Boys need men to model for them manhood!
If you want to raise a healthy man;
Get your son around healthy men.

Now I do want to say that I had a big mouth. I was the classic talker and instigator. To this day, I struggle with knowing when to talk and when to shut up! However, I felt like even the biggest loudmouth in the world shouldn't have to endure the kind of ridicule and teasing I did. My earliest memories are dominated by that horrible feeling of being talked about. I was teased about my middle name being Plato and my nickname being P.S., which stood for Prodigal Son (my aunt nicknamed me that), like the character in the Bible because I was always trying to get away, explore and do my own thing. Usually, I was the darkest Black kid in my circle, so I'd get called "Tar Baby", "Blacky" or "Black Sambo" because of my complexion. I would also get teased about being too short and for my "butt" being too big. Even girls would tease me, like the time I was walking up the stairs in school and a girl behind me shouted, "Damn, Glenn your ass is bigger than mine". I got teased about my weight, and my family's social status and the neighborhood I lived in. It seemed like I was the brunt of almost every joke you can imagine. You name it-I've heard it.

Now, don't get me wrong, I did my share of teasing too. But beyond what was normal, even for a "sensitive" kid, I just couldn't take it when it was done to me. I can't count the number of times I snuck away to cry because someone had hurt my feelings. And sometimes it was a lot more than my feelings that got hurt. Even though we moved around, it seemed like I was bullied and beat up at every school I attended. As early as second grade, I remember there was a fifth grader who decided I wasn't nice enough to his sister, so he tried to beat me up every day after school. The only thing that saved me was that I was faster than he was, and I could outrun this guy. But for weeks I found myself running home from school everyday just to avoid getting beat up. So, the adult translation of this behavior means that rather than standing and facing the music or truthfully sharing how I really feel I would take flight or run! As a result of this I became a major "People Pleaser". That is, rather than go through the door of confrontation and conflict, I found it easier to smile in your face than to tell you the truth and risk dealing with that "icky" feeling. As a mother raising a son, your challenge is, now that your son is all grown up, emotionally he is still a little boy and his wife can't understand his actions and reactions, even if her life depended on it. She asks herself, "Why is this man so passive?" Momma's Boys are passive because they have never seen a model of what it looks like for a strong man to stand up and fight for what he believes, in the right way. Therefore, we develop the dysfunctional habit of running *from* conflict and confrontation.

In middle school, I had a friend named Billy, who was easily twice my size. Billy was normally a quiet guy, but got a taste of popularity one day when he beat up a kid. He ended up turning on me and beat me up on a dare. So, Billy and I became rivals and he was always looking for a reason to fight me. This dude, who used to be peaceful, would just pick with me to get me to argue back. Well, it worked. I could always argue and talk trash with the best of them, but my fists couldn't keep up with my mouth! I lived in constant fear of physical confrontation.

One particular time, Billy and I were going at it on the bus. Forgetting that this guy had literally knocked a kid unconscious a few days before, I ran my famous mouth. "I'm going to kick your ass as soon as we get off this bus." Remember guys, I can't fight, what the hell was I thinking! Well the bus stopped and this time my pride wouldn't let me run away. All I remember was that he pushed me down from behind and started punching. I didn't fight back or anything. I just curled up like a turtle going into his shell. It was terrible. I remember my only goal was to not let him hit me in my face. Well, fortunately for my survival, his father drove by and saw his son beating the daylights out of someone two to three times smaller. "Billy get off of him, RIGHT NOW!!" Well, fortunately for me he obeyed his father and got up. I stayed there for a minute, first, because I wasn't sure if he was going to really leave me alone, but secondly, I could hear all the laughing and snickering little comments from the kids that lived in my neighborhood. They were saying stuff like, "that's what he gets", "he got his ass whipped", "I bet you he'll keep his mouth shut the next time and he ain't nothing but a lil' punk". I slowly got up, already utterly humiliated, to now see what seemed like the whole neighborhood standing around laughing at me. It took quite some time before that shame and humiliation went away.

I could go on and on with story after story about how I got "punked," because those are truly just a couple of stories out of many. My point is not so much that I went *through* this, but that there was no one in my life to teach me how to stand up for myself the right way. My identity began to be shaped as someone who either ran away, or stood there and got "punked". There were times that I'd tell my mother what was happening, but all she could do was hold me and tell me it would be okay. When I was younger, she dried my tears over the teasing I experienced because I was dark skinned. She would say "That's okay baby, the blacker the berry, the sweeter the juice."

Now, that's cute for a toddler, but it doesn't cut it for a twelve or thirteen-year-old boy who's being bullied daily. I needed someone to help me learn *how* to defend myself. I needed someone to explain to me what I now know, which is that *you don't have to beat everyone up to let the bullies know that it's no fun to pick on you.*

I needed someone to step in and say "Time out. What's going on? Why are you becoming everyone's punching bag? Why are you running home all the time?"

In other words, *I didn't need to be coddled.* I needed to be taught how to control my mouth, stand up for myself, and make better decisions. Yet coddling is what most mothers do, because that's what comes naturally to them. And, as I've already said and will probably say a lot more, what comes naturally a lot of times *isn't even close to good enough.*

TWO
Lovers and Haters

I remember it like it was yesterday. It was a Saturday in February in Maryland. Needless to say, it was freezing cold. I'm nervous. I'm trying not to show it, but I keep messing with my tie and checking my hair in the mirror. My dad is late as usual, but this time it's not a matter of being late to the movies: the ceremony is about to get started without him. I'm getting married!

So, on the biggest day of my life, I'm thinking to myself how this man always does this. He always promises that he's going to do something or be somewhere and lets me down. My father finally shows up "fashionably late". You know, "CP time". My mother has been in place with the other guests from the beginning. She's being great, smiling and hugging everyone, but in her heart she knows this is a big mistake. I didn't understand until years later why my mother asked me several times and in several different ways, "what's the rush?" She's not pregnant, is she? No ma, I answered, we're in love! However, the timing was off and I think my mother knew it. She wasn't trying to control me but she kept asking me "are you sure"? It would be years before I could answer that question-years of pain that comes from a life of trial and error. I now know that I was rushing to marry because I was tired of hearing in church "you're going to Hell for fornicating"! Fornicating means having sex outside of marriage. Now, you couple this with having an addiction to using women to fill the emptiness in my heart. It's easy to understand why getting married at twenty was the answer, I thought, to having sex without the guilt and avoiding going to hell in the process. If only I knew how very wrong I was!

My new wife was just nineteen, and neither of us had any idea how much this mistake was going to cost us. What do you get when you mix two immature people with wild emotions, crazy dreams and no plan? You get what my friend Deron Cloud calls the "Boyfriend Girlfriend Thang". Although the marriage license said I became a husband on that day, I was just a boy marrying a girl. Neither of us had a clue.

Born to Mess Up

Unknowingly, both my parents set me up to mess up as a husband. I don't say that out of anger or to blame them. It is simply a fact. Did they do it on purpose? Did they sit down one day and say, "Let's do everything we can to make Glenn grow up to be the kind of man that will mistreat his wife and fail as a husband." Of course not, but that's precisely the point I want you to get. They didn't do it on purpose because they weren't thinking at all about making me into anything. They were doing "what they had to do," which most of the time translated into being away from me physically or giving me easy, comfortable answers to my questions. I realize this could sound harsh, perhaps even ungrateful and unsympathetic. After all, my mom had to work, right? So, it's not like she was lounging around at a resort while I was getting beat up in school.

But, my purpose in writing this book is not to tell you what you already know. You know that it is hard to raise children, especially by yourself. You already know that there are never enough hours in the day or dollars in the bank. But, do you know what is going on inside your son's head? Do you know what he's thinking, what he's feeling and what you can do about it? Without condemning anyone, I just want to open your eyes to the perspective of a Momma's Boy. I can also tell you how the story will come out if you don't start thinking now about the kind of man you are teaching your son to be.

A Momma's Boy, in my experience, grows up one of two ways: a "lover" of women or a "hater" of women. Lovers become so comfortable with the company of women that their mannerisms are often expressed like that of a woman. This does NOT mean they are attracted to men, but many times it will cause them to question their own sexuality. This leaves countless young men vulnerable to those who would aggressively try to pursue a homosexual relationship with them. You probably know someone who has fallen prey to that kind of thing. The bottom line is: *lovers are more comfortable being "one of the girls."* Their dependence on their mothers has shaped them to want to be just like her.

Momma's Boys that become "haters" are a different story all together. Haters develop levels of disrespect, distrust, and downright contempt for women that can approach sociopathic levels. On the surface, the hater appears to be the most charming, loving, thoughtful boyfriend you'd ever want to meet. However, in most cases the reality is that he is a master manipulator and uses his words to get whatever he wants. Contrary to popular belief, it isn't just sex he wants. Sex may just be the final stage of the conquest. Haters seduce women to themselves by showing interest in them to get them to open up emotionally. Haters then use this insight into her mind and heart to dominate her more effectively. She reveals more and more of herself, while he stays completely closed, holding all the cards. The real tragedy is that most men do this, at least in the beginning, completely unaware of what is really happening. If asked the Hater would tell you with the utmost sincerity that it's simply who he is, not what he does. However, subtly he has had years to perfect his craft.

I remember being as young as ten, asking my mom questions about the female body. What's a period? How are babies born? Of course she resisted telling me at first, but I begged and pleaded until she gave in, telling me way more than I had any business knowing at that age. I want to stress that this was *not* normal healthy curiosity. My mother was completely unaware that by the time I'd begun to ask these probing questions, I'd been looking at porno magazines, masturbating, and having sex with girls in my neighborhood. I was gathering information that would later help me manipulate girls. I was growing to be a

Hater, and I was becoming very good at the game.

Pop Quiz

Two years into my marriage, the real test began. It was a test I wouldn't just fail once. No, this was a test I would fail over and over again for the next twelve years. We've all had that math exam we blew, and if we studied real hard the next time, we could bring that grade back up. But my test had only one question: Could I and would I be faithful to my wife?

I was in the military at the time. I'd sent my wife back to Maryland to live with her mother. The idea was that she could get a job until my enlistment was over-in six months. I was stationed in New Jersey, but I returned home on the weekends to see my wife. Things were going pretty well at first. Separation was hard, but it made sense to me at the time. While I was preparing to leave the military, my wife was helping to prepare the civilian life that we would soon begin together. It was a logical plan and it should have worked. However, "logical" only works for healthy and functional people.

The signs of my sickness finally showed up one day when I was leaving work and saw a car with rims that I admired. Without thinking twice, I left a note on the car, "Really liked the rims—call me with info on where I can get some for my car". I wasn't ready for a woman to call me. Now *you* know where this story is going, but I didn't. I was twenty-two and my wife was one-hundred fifty miles away. And here I was, talking on the phone to a woman with a red sports car about how I wanted to purchase rims for my car. Now a man with some sense would have gotten the information and left her alone. But, I didn't do that. Instead of remembering those vows I took that cold Saturday in February and thinking about my wife working to establish a life for me when I left the military, I started calling the "new" woman.

This is a classic mistake of a Hater. The question is never whether something is wise or right. The question is, "Does this make me feel good, emotionally or physically?" You see, my upbringing had failed to give me the wisdom and self-control I would need to stay out of adultery. It had been about finding the quickest way to soothe my pain or quiet my whining. So, when I grew up, I looked for the quickest way to soothe my pain or quiet my inner complaints.

This lady was older and she wasn't even gorgeous by a long shot. But, this was about more than just animal lust, like some affairs are. She paid attention to me. She was nurturing and understanding. I liked talking to her and eventually I liked going out to lunch with her, then dinner, then the movies. I should also add that I was seriously endangering my career, because she was the wife of a high-ranking non-commissioned officer. So, I could have been arrested for fraternizing with her. But, for six months, I lied to myself, my wife and everyone else about what was going on with me. I learned quickly with this woman that all the practice I'd had lying to my mom growing up, worked. Like the time that I was leaving the mall driving my mothers' new car, and accidently hit a pole. Well, the story I told her was that I was walking out of the mall, only to notice that someone must have backed into the car because it didn't look like this (damaged) when I went into the store. Well she bought it "hook, line and sinker". I had begun to craft and refine the "skill set of deceit" at that early age and now, I was using it to pull off concealing an affair and destroying everything that should be important to me.

HERE'S A THOUGHT:
Children do what you do,
more than what you say.
If you want your son to "do" different;
Then show him the difference.

It's All About Me

As a mother, you already know that all children are born selfish. They do not automatically know how to be considerate and put others before themselves in a way that will help them cultivate healthy, successful relationships. Unselfishness is the kind of character that must be deliberately instilled by dedicated role models-the kind that first demonstrates character in their own lives.

Now, what I'm about to say next may seem a little conflicting, but stay with me a minute further. You can make a kid selfish and self-centered by ignoring him and neglecting him AND you also can do it by spoiling him, coddling him, and indulging his immaturity. Those seem like two opposite behaviors, right? But really they are both cheap, easy ways to deal with having a kid around. (1) Pretend he's not there, or (2) just give him what he wants so he'll shut up. Overworked moms have it rough and many times don't have the energy to do more than that. However, let my life serve as a warning to you: If you don't put in the time and effort that it will take to teach and train your son *how* to do right and *why* he must do right, you and your son will pay a terrible price.

I didn't understand then, but I was addicted to being the center of attention. Although they didn't set out to warp me, I remember my aunts; both my grandmothers and my mother's friends were always making over me in an "over-the-top" kind of way. So, whenever opportunities arose to get attention, especially from a woman, I would go on a binge, just like an alcoholic. Then, just like other addicts, this tendency to binge became a cancerous emotional growth, slowly spreading and killing every relationship that meant anything to me during my early adult years. So, even though I was married, I started living single. Living single is just that – you live with the constant attitude and behaviors that shouts, "I am the only one that matters." It was all about me. When a boy is catered to by his mother and made to feel like all he has to do is "whimper" and momma is going to be there, he begins to develop a completely selfish outlook on life.

He says to himself, *"It's all about me"*. And, as a man, such a mindset can become detrimental to his relationships. If momma is always there to grant my every "whim", she is teaching me that my wife must also do the same and if she won't, "I'll just throw a fit, act out, and have a temper tantrum or whatever you want to call it. Acting out as an adult is very different than acting out as a child.

ACTING OUT CHART:

<u>CHILD</u>	<u>ADULT</u>
- He Pouts	- He yells
- He whines and complains	- He leaves
- He goes to his room	- He shuts you out
- He begs and pleads	- He manipulates
- He cries	- He has an attitude
- He sneaks (in secret)	- He takes it (openly)

I did *what* I wanted *when* and *where* and *how* I wanted, just like I had done growing up. I was a Momma's Boy that just had to have his way all the time. Where does that level of selfishness come from? What in a man produces a complete disregard for the feelings and well-being of those closest to him, especially the women? What causes a married man to calculate striking up a conversation with an old girlfriend, flirt with her, and set a time and date when they will get together, specifically to have sex? *It's his conviction that he is the only one who matters.*

The next several years involved many nights of getting home way too late, only to lie about things like, "getting a flat and having to walk to a gas station to get help". I concocted the most detailed elaborate stories about various uncontrollable circumstances, when the sad truth was that I was off having a great time with a woman who couldn't stand my wife and would screw me just to be spiteful!

But the lesson I learned (much too late) was that by doing things that hurt the people closest to me, I was also destroying myself. So, as a result, I systematically learned how to hate myself.

> **HERE'S A THOUGHT:**
> *If a man can't love and respect himself;*
> *Know this*
> *You ain't got nothin' coming!*

Failure Breeds Failure

I realize that my parents failed me in some very important ways because of failures during their own upbringings. Again, I want to emphasize that I am not saying any of this to condemn anyone. I am saying this because it is reality, and if no one has the courage to lay these things out on the table, we'll keep repeating the mistakes of the past. I was born to parents who were just 19, naïve and immature. What can you expect from a couple of teenagers who got pregnant and then got married to "make it right"? In many ways, they did the best they knew. My father never knew his father and his mother, doing the best she knew, was on public assistance as long as I can remember, as were many of the people in her South Baltimore neighborhood.

Like me, my dad was the only boy in a family full of girls. He was raised by women and never had the stable influence of a consistent, faithful father in his life. When it came to being the oldest and only boy, he too enjoyed being the center of attention. His mother loved him, protected him, and even lied for him when she thought it necessary. My dad was very close to his sisters too, and to this day, he always looks out for them. My father finished most of his growing up while in the army, eventually fighting a war he didn't understand. So, now I see that he couldn't teach me what he didn't know. And though I can honestly say I don't blame him for all the problems I've had and that I believe he did the best he could, I will say, however, that my father's failures at fatherhood have had distinct and lasting consequences in my own life.

My mother's life wasn't perfect either. She was the second to the youngest of four other siblings, having the influence of both her parents in the home. But not a whole lot of individual time and attention was available, since they both spent many hours working outside the home to keep their children clothed and fed, with a roof over their heads. Like her dad, my mom was very artistic and creative, but also very quiet. She, too, had the darkest skin in her family and felt insecure because she was teased. But there was something amazing in her that wanted to come out and express itself. However, from my little boy perspective, it only showed itself in her tendency to be controlling.

My grandfather always had several jobs because he believed in providing for his family. He was also a pastor and my mother tells me that teaching God's Word gave him the greatest joy. I remember my mother telling me of his passion for education and the joy he felt when educating others.

He was a good man, stretched *way* too thin. Despite my grandfather's best intentions, it was impossible to keep everything going without something suffering. In my experience, it's almost always the kids that pay the heaviest price. Growing up without an informed and available parent also has its price and my mother found that out firsthand. Years later, I would learn that growing up with an overworked, uninformed, misunderstood and confused mother is the perfect atmosphere for producing a Momma's Boy and, in my case, a woman hater.

Most people are products of their environment. People do what they see others do, people also do what they know - not what they believe. My culture raised me and it taught me, "If it feels good do it". I'll later explain how I became addicted to "feeling good" and how sex became my drug of choice. My sexual addiction, which later led to adultery, wasn't my only failure as a husband, but it illustrates perfectly what was wrong with me. I loved to have sex with women, but I had a complete disdain for their value as people. Remember any man who will have sex with you outside of marriage doesn't respect or care about you. Any man who will cheat on his wife with you doesn't love you anymore than he loves the woman he's lying to. He's just enjoying you for right now.

That's how I was. I was addicted to using women to soothe my pain. I was enjoying myself for the moment. In my struggle to assert my manhood over my youthful insecurities, I was ruining the lives of women, as well as my own. This was all possible because I was left to my environment, to my culture, and ultimately to myself to figure it all out.

HERE'S A THOUGHT:

A man who finds his significance in women has the ability to destroy that woman's life.

THREE
He's Out of Control!

Most of us have some experience with credit card debt. Most of us know what it feels like when you can't really afford that outfit or that new TV, so you put it on the card or you finance it. You tell yourself you'll pay it off when you get paid. Well, payday comes and goes and you really had to get those new tires after that blowout on the highway. Some of us also can remember being too tired to cook on a Friday and so pizza was just a "little treat". Before you knew it, you'd paid for that TV and that outfit thirty-five times and all because you wouldn't set a little money aside each month and *wait* for what you wanted.

I'm not trying to give you a lecture on financial management, but I am trying to show you a principle here. With just about anything in life, you have to be willing to make some short-term sacrifices to accomplish long-term goals. If not, you will pay for things many times over. Nowhere is this truer than when raising a child. *If you invest the time and energy and sacrifice in your son while he's growing up*, even when you feel like you have nothing left to give, you can steer him in the right direction. If not, you will pay for the sacrifices you weren't willing to make and you will pay with interest.

Protect Him or Lose Him

Now I want to talk to you for a minute about what your son really needs. I've already said I'm not writing this book to tell you what you already know. You know he needs food, clothes, and a safe place to live and you know that providing those things can seem impossible at times. However, I want to talk to you about some things he needs just as much as food. *The first is protection.*

Protecting a child is one of the most basic duties of a parent. Even wild animals protect their young. Everyone knows the best way to get killed by a mother bear or mother lion is to mess with her cubs. It's easy for us to understand that daughters need protection from predators who would steal their emotional or physical innocence, but I'm here to tell you that boys need that protection too.

I told you in the last chapter that I started questioning my mom about sex at a very young age. Well, she eventually gave into my pleading and before I knew it, she was talking to me like I was one of her girlfriends. The problem was, this girlfriend had a penis and he was trying to put it in as many girls as possible. You see what she didn't know, but should have suspected, was by the time I was asking her technical questions, I had been engaging in sexual activity for years. That's right, before a boy should even begin "discovering" girls, I was already experimenting with sex. I would use the information she gave me to appear knowledgeable to the girls I was preying on. All this happened because I did not have a parent who knew how to protect my innocence.

My first sexual encounter happened when I was about six. A bunch of us were over a friend's house just playing around. Then my cousin, who was about ten, says, "Why don't you "do it" to her?" He was talking about a little girl who was just seven years old at the time.

"NO WAY!" I refused. "If you don't, I'm going to tell your mother that you went outside when you wasn't supposed to," he threatened. "Awwh come on don't tell her that, I'll get in trouble," I protested. "Well, do it to her with the pants down and I won't tell," he promised, smiling that he got his way.

I knew the little girl very well. She lived across the street from my cousins' house and we were friends. Whenever my sister and I would come up to spend the weekend with my cousins we would all play together. It was just innocent play, but on that day we would both lose something we could never get back.

The older kids told her to go into the bedroom. Because this little girl was what we called "hot" or "fast," she went willingly and took her pants off. I went in, took my pants down, jumped on top of her and started "humping." Of course there was no penetration, but did you know there were seven-year-old girls that would do that? My mother clearly must not have known that either. I went along with it and it felt good in a way, but I was way too young to understand what was happening. The girl never complained, but neither of us knew we were really victims.

Neither did we know that while it was going on, my cousin snuck in the room and took a picture of us. He used a Polaroid camera, so it popped right out after it was taken. As soon as it developed, he ran around the house showing it to all the kids that were there that day. They threatened to show it to my mother and my cousin would use that picture against me to get me to "do it" many more times after that day. This was decades ago, but I can still remember it like it was yesterday. This incident pushed me into a life of isolation and sexual addiction that I struggled with for years.

How did it happen? We were kids just playing around, but we completely lacked sufficient adult supervision. Now I can hear a lot of people object, saying that you can't watch your children twenty-four hours a day. However, as a parent myself, I honestly believe you have an obligation to know where your children are physically, emotionally, and socially. This includes knowing whom they're with and evaluating those people to make sure they will not negatively influence your child or victimize him in any way.

Who are your children exposed to on a regular basis? Do you really know what they are like? I was exposed to tons of things I shouldn't have been, all because I was hanging out, unsupervised, with older kids, some of whom were my relatives! Several times before the incident I just described, an older female cousin would ask her younger brother and me to do the "Hawaii 5-0." That was when we would take our pants down and act like we were playing the guitar, strumming our penises to the tune of the TV show theme. At four and five years old, we thought this was hilarious. So did all the other older kids who watched and laughed. This kind of thing happened all the time, but those incidents wouldn't have happened if we had been properly supervised. When you've been doing that kind of thing ever since you can remember, by the time your older cousin says "I want ya'll to do it with the pants down" you know exactly what that person means. We were damaging our sexuality before it had even begun to develop and the grown-ups closest to us had no clue, so they didn't say anything to stop it.

My sexual appetite over the next few years would become insatiable. As early as eight years old, I would look at trashed porn magazines, which belonged to my mother's boyfriend. I found them in our kitchen trashcan. I even tore out some of the pages and tacked them to the walls of the tree fort my friends and I had made in the woods. My friends and I would take in images of "hard core pornography" almost every day during the summer. As far as I knew, not one single adult knew about our steady diet of perversion, especially our parents.

Now, just so you know, I am not exposing these painful, haunting memories just to make you sick to your stomach or to make you feel sorry for me. I want you to see what happens when you as a mom raising a boy singlehandedly do not take every available measure to be aware of your son's activities and protect him physically, spiritually, and emotionally. You can buy him all the designer clothes, shoes, Xboxes, PSPs, keep his hair tight, and get that bike he begs for, but if you don't protect his mind, body and soul, it's all for nothing. You'll be raising a well-dressed kid whose soul is rotting away inside.

In my own experiences, I've found that most adults are way too uninvolved with their children. Listen to me, sister, "Your son needs you." Sure, since you're single, he needs you to provide, but he also needs your presence-consistently. He needs it in different ways at different ages. Your presence in his life will protect him in more ways than you'll ever know.

Communicate or Lose Him

Now, no mother naturally would suspect her children's blood cousins, especially those only a few years older, would exploit her children. That is why YOU MUST PAY ATTENTION to your children AND their friends. There are almost always clear signs that your kids are involved in something harmful -

signs that you will miss if you are asleep at the wheel. What do I mean by that?

For some parents, it could be overlooking a simple comment that your child makes in the back seat of the car while you are driving him to school. For a moment, a thought flashes through your mind, "Where did that come from?" But you keep on driving, thinking about the millions of other things that you have going on. Later, if you remember it at all, you go into denial, thinking, "That can't be what they really meant." Trust me, when you fall asleep at the wheel guarding your kids, there is no way to avoid the crash! And from this "accident" there will be injuries and maybe even fatalities.

Still other parents may recognize something's not quite right, but make the fatal mistake of *interrogating* their child. They jump all over him, ask invasive questions, and then tell him how dumb he sounds after he tries to answer. For some reason, mothers who do this think they are being really tough and strong, thinking to themselves "this toughness is what he needs." Yet in the end, this approach will virtually guarantee that he won't open up to her again for a long time.

What I want to challenge you to do is stop and think. Think about what you could say that would make your son want to tell you more. Remember, before you can address a problem, you've got to know what it is. You need information. Seize those moments because eventually he'll let something slip out! Ask a non-threatening question like "What did you think about that?" or "Oh really? What are those guys like?"

Keep your voice calm and remember, *you* are the adult.

I do acknowledge that a lot of the "normal" times for interacting with our children are under heavy attack. More and more families don't have or even make the time for having dinner together. There is something sacred about this time at the table, sharing a meal without hurrying through it to get to the next thing on our To-Do lists. Instead, its rush, rush, and rush. "Wake up, or you'll be late for school!" Meanwhile, you're on your way out the door so you won't be late for work. He spends his breakfast alone with the TV and you spend yours either at the corner coffee shop or doughnut place, in the car or on the bus.

When you get home, he's already out the door, trying to find that "feeling of family" at a friend's house or playing a sport. Of course, you have to get a shower and get out of the house to a second job or to church or whatever else you have going on. At your home, family time" doesn't exist. The point I'm making is that when you don't have what I call "*purposed face-time*" with your kids, you are giving them over to their world of TV, friends, and music - external forces you have little to no control over are now your son's primary influences. At this point, he is "out of control" because he's beyond your control.

HERE'S A THOUGHT:

How often do you spend time quality time with your son?
Before you answer, what would he say?
If it's not enough, spend more.
He's worth it.

Unfortunately, by the time most parents figure this out, years have passed and crisis is "king". You wonder, "How did all this happen? How did I lose my son?" While you were busy doing "what you had to do," you were losing him.

I was that little boy who grew up having to figure everything out on my own. (Maybe you've seen what I went through in your own son). I couldn't communicate what I felt without becoming angry. I was constantly anxious about basic activities and threw myself into anything that would help me escape life. At first, it was TV and sports. When I was older, it was clothes, money, or hustling. We actually introduce our kids to these things in our ignorance. Then again, sometimes we do it indirectly. Instead of teaching them to talk about what they fear and feel, we teach them to quiet their anxiety with addictive behaviors.

In the remaining chapters, I will suggest some strategies to help you break this cycle. However, before you can fix something, you have to spend quality time diagnosing what's going on. You have to be able to communicate.

Confront Him or Lose Him

Her name was Krystal and she was my first girlfriend. It was 4th grade, and we had moved out of the city and to the suburbs. The neighborhood was nice; my mom got a job working in the federal government at a nearby military base. Environmentally, it wasn't what we were used to, but it was okay. I remember the school didn't have walls in the classrooms, which I thought was cool. The relaxed structure fit my sanguine personality, which is energetic and outgoing. I could literally see into an entire row of classrooms. That's how I first saw Krystal, she was very light-skinned, with wavy hair and I thought she was as cute as a button. I don't remember a lot of details; I just remember that I just had to talk to her.

Before I knew it, I was striking up conversations with her in the hall, or the cafeteria or wherever I could. That's how I found out that she lived within walking distance of my house. Talk about convenient! This meant I could see her in <u>and</u> out of school. TOUCHDOWN!!!!!

Now you may be thinking, "How cute"-"Puppy love, a first crush." But it could never be that innocent for someone who had grown up like I did. You see, I'd already been introduced to "sexual pleasure". As I've told you, I was scheming at nine years old how to get with Krystal. I was a fourth grader, trying to figure out how far I could get with this little girl. She was funny and really sweet, but I could never be content to just laugh with her and enjoy her company.

Finally, she invited me to come over her house to play. The problem was that I knew my mother would not approve of this. You see, it wasn't that my mom didn't have standards or rules for me. She just wasn't involved enough in my life to make sure they were enforced. So of course, I made up a lie about where I was going and why. I don't even remember what I said, but it worked. Mom let me go. This was when I learned to "work" a female. My mom, unknowingly, was giving me all the practice I would need to be a deceptive adulterer later in life.

I was having a great time at Krystal's house and soon it was time for dinner. Now how did I know her mother was cooking fried chicken? To this day, it's my favorite (I can still smell it cooking). Her mother asked me to stay for dinner and when I agreed, she asked me if it was okay with my mom. So of course, I had to lie again. My mother had no idea where I really was. Whatever lie I had told her, she was satisfied and didn't follow through to make sure I was where I said I would be. So ladies, don't just take a child's word, no matter how much you know or like the child, call their parent.

So, I stayed and had dinner. By the time we finished, it was getting pretty dark outside. Now the rule in our house was that you had to be in the house before the streetlights come on. Remember those days? My challenge now became how to explain being out so late. In fact, I ended up staying out so late that my mom had progressed from being annoyed to being worried and then to going out to search for me. I don't know how long or where she actually searched, but by the time I came walking up to the court where I lived, I heard people calling my name. The closer I got, the louder the voices. It was completely dark, I was nine years old and it sounded like the entire neighborhood was looking for me. Hearing all this, I knew I was going to be in big trouble. I needed a new plan to get out of this jam.

Now remember, lying was starting to come naturally to me. I figured I had, somehow, to get around to the back of my house un-detected by the neighbors who were roaming the streets yelling my name. That way, I could make it look like I was coming out of the woods behind our house. I could say I was busy looking for frogs and didn't realize the streetlights had come on. What can I say? I was nine.

Well, believe it or not, it worked. Someone saw me coming out of the woods and asked me where I'd been. He told me everyone had been looking for me and that my mother was worried sick. They all thought something terrible had happened to me. This was my first chance to practice my story. I warmed up by convincing others before selling it to my mother. Once I finally got in the house, I found my mother in the bathroom crying, thinking something terrible had happened to me. When she first saw me, all she could do was cry and hug me, and thank God that I was safe.

Once she realized that I was okay, of course, the questions started to come. Where were you! Where have you been! The joy of finding me safe had vanished and she wanted some answers. And at nine years old, looking at the only adult who had ever been there for me-in the deepest pain and anguish possible-I told my "frog story" with the straightest face and my most convincingly innocent voice. At first, she looked at me like I was crazy. "Frogs?" she said. "What?" Completely confused, she ordered me to my room so she could pull herself together. Now after a scare like that, you would hope your son would learn a lesson. So what did I learn? Did I learn how horrible it feels to scare someone you love? Did I learn that my own carelessness could devastate other people's lives? No. I learned that if I could get away with this stupid story that I thought of in two desperate seconds, the sky was the limit and she would believe anything I told her. I had no idea that the ability to manipulate would be so intoxicating.

I was even becoming a liar and a manipulator in elementary school. I could make up the craziest stories and people would believe it. Worse yet, adults would believe it! When your son lies, you can't allow him to get away with it. Now, I will be the first to admit that catching him and confronting him takes a tremendous amount of patience and energy. Most parents don't discipline effectively because it takes more energy to discipline than to yell and even more energy to execute "corporal punishment" (to beat the black off of him, just kidding I mean to take a belt to his bottom)! You know, that magical answer to everything in most Black families: "Just beat his ass!" You need to confront him and get him to understand the effect of what he has done. He needs to understand that *lying is wrong* and *why it is wrong*. You must teach him that the trust of other people is a precious thing.

HERE'S A THOUGHT:

Fussing with your son doesn't work;
Never has and never will.
What does work is consequences.

He needs to know the difference between being an honorable man and being a common thug. Then finally, you must enforce lasting consequences that will cause him to *feel* the loss. Maybe that includes controlled corporal punishment, but you will probably need to remove the phone, videogames, TV privileges and/or time spent with friends for a significant amount of time. We call it, "The shut down", using the loss of what's important to him as a tool to get him to understand and own the consequences of his actions.

Now it should be obvious that you will have no credibility to do this if your son has seen you lie or deceive. Most parents eventually learn that *what they do and the life they live* in front of their children *speaks much louder than most of what they actually say.* In the next chapter, I'll share with you why it was so easy for me to lie and why it was so hard for my mom to do anything about it.

FOUR
Under The Influence

I've talked to you about being asleep at the wheel and missing those crucial moments when your son opens up. I also have given you some insight into what's going on in his head and in his life. And if you're a single mother working hard to make ends meet, those moments are absolutely vital to (1) understanding your son, (2) identifying the "Momma's Boy" tendencies and (3) catching it before it grows out of control. Still, I want to encourage you that you have far more influence over your son than you think. However, you need to be aware that this influence can be used for both good and bad.

Most women are unaware of the power they have, especially within their households. We tend to think of powerful women as those who either make a lot of money in a glamorous career or harness their sex appeal to keep their men whipped, you know running around in "tights". However, there are other ways you influence your family, especially your son. Those ways may not be obvious, but in the long run they have a more profound effect. You influence those in your household as a nurturer, a caregiver, a teacher, and a disciplinarian. Your provision and your love give you profound influence over those you take care of. In one of his best-selling books "The 21 Irrefutable Laws of Leadership" John Maxwell says, "Leadership is influence, nothing more and nothing less." You are a leader in your son's life.

If you are heading the household without a husband, then all the leadership responsibilities fall on you. You can talk about how hard it is and you are right. You can talk about how it isn't fair and it isn't. However, none of that changes the fact that everything rests squarely on your shoulders alone. It's your job. When you understand and embrace that, you'll realize that your son will follow you. The question is where are you leading him?

What You Don't Know Can Kill Him

One of the greatest things that any mother needs to remember is that she is raising a future adult. This is a huge job. Unlike becoming a doctor, lawyer, beautician or maybe even a mechanic, you don't need a degree, a license or certification to get this job. Some of you got the job by having sex one time. So, if you were never taught or didn't take the time to educate yourself for this job beforehand, you've got some catching up to do and you had better take it seriously.

My mother was in a situation like many of you: after a failed marriage, she found herself raising two kids alone. This wasn't what she dreamed of as a little girl and it sure wasn't what she expected when she married my father. Yet, it quickly became her reality. And, like many of you, she woke up one day realizing it was something that she was not fully equipped to do. Unfortunately for us, she couldn't carve out enough time between working two jobs and going to college in the evening (so she could get a job paying the salary that her two jobs paid) to take care of us. My mom would tell us that too many times she caught herself driving asleep with her eyes open! Most of the time, she was just too physically tired to even do what she knew was right to do. And sadly, my sister and I paid the biggest price for her fatigue.

[1]*"Some mothers raise their daughters and mother their sons,"* says Dr. Kunjufu, I now understand what that means. Most mothers at least put thought into preparing their daughters for what life will demand of them. Women can usually relate to their daughters because they are female. For the most part, mothers understand what their daughter

---

[1] Footnote: [1] Article entitled "How Parents view the way sons and daughters view their dates, spouses and the world" – Parenting (Ebony, June 2003 by Lynn Norment, Kevin Chappell)

are going through, how they feel and what they want. My mother could relate to my sister because she once was a little girl. On the other hand, I was another story. By my mom's own admission, she had "no idea what to do with me". From the time I came out of the womb, full of testosterone, I was "something else" as she would say. I can bet that most of you understand what I'm talking about. Boys, especially many Black boys, are super-aggressive. Why? Boys we are designed to be hunters and gatherers. "Parenting" can quickly turn into fighting to control that aggression. At first, Mom, you win because you are bigger, but you don't realize that you are raging against your son's inner nature.

If your only goal is to control his behavior, you will force him to develop unnaturally. Your goal should be to teach him to control himself. That is what makes a real man- not an absence of aggression - but complete control over it. This is what I'm still learning.

Now some moms may have grown up with brothers or some other influence that helps them understand boys a little better than most. However, others lacking those kinds of experiences may have much to learn if you want to raise your son successfully. You must take time to educate yourself about what your son is going through at each stage of his life. I have included a short reading list at the end of this book for you to tackle. However, one of your critical needs will be to communicate with people who can help you raise your son. Do you know anyone who has successfully raised a son to become a responsible young man? If so, she may be able to offer some insight on specific things your son is going through. Don't be too proud to ask for help. Being prideful will leave you stumbling around in the dark when you don't have too and it will teach your son to do the same. Remember, you are already an influencer. The question is whether most of your influence will make your son into a mature and responsible man or an out-of-control mess of a man on wheels.

My behavior reflected my mother's strengths and flaws and it revealed all the areas she had left unchallenged and unexplored in her own life. When nobody tells you certain things, you have to figure everything out on your own through trial and error, which is a very expensive way to learn. For example, if you have never been taught how to create a personal budget, create financial goals, or control your spending habits, you'll just keep spending what you have as soon as you get it. You may work just as hard as others, but at the end of the year, you'll have nothing to show for it. In contrast, someone else who has learned the skills you missed will earn the same money and get further ahead in life. In the meantime, you'll try this and then try that, but find yourself ten years later still trying to figure out how to get out of debt while everyone else, or so it seems, is planning for their retirement.

Now think about your son. If *you* don't teach him how to listen and excel in school, how will he know how? If *you* don't anticipate the problems he's going to have with his friends and teach him how to respond to pressure and criticism, how will he figure it out? Raising your son means you are determining what he needs to know and making sure he knows it. To make sure he knows it, you have to make sure you know it first. If you leave it up to the school or the other adults in his life, then you are rolling the dice on how your son will turn out. You are indirectly and ultimately teaching him to raise himself.

"If you can control a man's thinking, you do not have to worry about his action. When you determine what a man shall think, you do not have to concern yourself about what he will do. If you make a man feel that he is inferior, you

do not have to compel him to accept an inferior status, for he will seek it himself. If you make a man think that he is justly an outcast, you do not have to order him to the back door. He will go without being told; and if there is no back door, his very nature will demand one." - Carter G. Woodson, The Mis-Education of the Negro

My mother's mis-education or lack of sufficient knowledge about how to raise a son resulted in both of us paying a dear price. Now it's easy to tell your son he's great and that he'd better not let anyone look down on him. However, it's another thing entirely to give him the character qualities he'll need to actually accomplish great things.

Ask yourself: What is shaping your son's thinking? How are you ensuring that you have the right information to steer him on the right path?

Think about your own life and education. Do you want your son to know more or less than you knew at his age? Do you want him to make better or worse choices than you did? *If you don't invest the time and energy to learn what you need to know and what he needs to know*, you are guaranteeing he'll make all the same mistakes you made, plus more of his own.

HERE'S A THOUGHT:

No parent is perfect.

But if we can be authentic, vulnerable, and show humility we will give our children a fighting chance.

What You Do

You have influence over where your son goes, what he owns and even what he eats. You must use that influence wisely. *What you do with your time, your money, and your energy* should show the right priorities to your son. You can <u>tell</u> him he's important all day long, but if your time and energy go to other things, he won't feel that he is important to you. By the time I was six or seven years old, I was already closing myself off from my mom because in my opinion her attention was too focused on other areas.

What decisions are you making that are shaping your son's life? Do you take him to the library or drop him at the movies? Is your house filled with books, DVDs, or video games? When you have a spare moment, does he see you reading, watching TV, or laying around doing nothing?

Is his stomach filled with fruits, vegetables, and whole grains, or just some fast food you picked up on your way home from work? If you want your son to grow up to make good choices, you've got to make sure you are making good choices too.

Remember, a real man doesn't lack the aggression that may drive you crazy in a three-year-old; he just learns to successfully control it. Now I have to ask you, how well do you control your own emotions? Do you think you can teach your son self-control if you yell and scream at him to vent your own frustration? Your first step toward successfully influencing your son toward maturity is showing him what a self-controlled adult looks like.

A lot of people think a Momma's Boy is a boy that's too close to his mother. That's not always true; a Momma's Boy is a boy that *functions emotionally* like a female. When you're a boy that spends a considerable amount of time around only females and don't have healthy relationships with males, it's very likely that you'll pick up the habits and responses of the females in your home, and those whom you spent time with during your formative years. If you and the other women around your son were manipulative and untrusting, then your son will absorb that. I know, because I did. I learned to be charming and how to get my way. By hanging around women, I learned what buttons to push to get whatever I wanted from her.

I began exercising my "feminine-manipulation" skills very early on. I remember one time in elementary school our class was walking down the hallway in single-file. Remember those days? I was behaving just fine until a girl decided to cut in front of me and we got into a little skirmish. I wound up telling this girl to, "Suck my **** (you fill in the blank!), and she went to tell the teacher.

Well, I had this particular teacher pegged as a classic "push-over." I knew all I had to do was deny the accusation and passionately explain why she was "lying on me," ideally producing some real tears. When the teacher questioned me, I pulled it off beautifully. SLAM-DUNK! I had this guy wrapped around my finger. I learned that approach by watching a bunch of manipulative emotional women. I never learned that a real man takes responsibility for his actions, owns up and takes his punishment. I never learned to, "take it like a man."

As a matter of fact, the more I observed the women in my life, the more of their *emotional* behavior I picked up. It is amazing to me that mothers think their own deceptive ways will not affect their children. So, if you want your son to respect women, you must be a woman who commands respect from men. You must have high moral standards for yourself, and teach your son to have the same. As a parent myself, I can promise you that the "Do as I say, not as I do" thing has never worked, and it never will.

Who You Are

Few things reflect who you are at your core more than your relationships. Remember, as you build a relationship with your son, he is also watching all your relationships with other people. And if you form a romantic relationship with a man, you can bet he is picking up on everything, no matter how well you think you're concealing it. You can sneak him out of the house before your child wakes up. You can lie to him and tell him it's none of his business. You can let the men bribe him and try to win his affection with gifts. But if there's something messed up going on, you can bet that you're influencing him for evil.

Why is it that single mothers who claim they can't find time to cook nutritious meals, or read to their son, or take him to the park or the library can still find time to date? The short answer is that they are trying to fill a void inside of themselves. This void may have been caused by situations that resulted in any number of emotional vacuums - from feelings of abandonment to low self-esteem.

I want to tell you honestly, when I was younger, the hardest part of watching my mom date was the fact that the men she dated weren't my father. They weren't violent drunks who would beat her up. Nor were they even mean, nasty, or controlling. But for me, they were living breathing reminders that my father was never coming back to us and that our family would never be whole again.

Now, I know there are a lot of people saying that there's no such thing as a "model family" and that any kind of arrangement is as good as any other. However, I'm here to tell you that to a young boy, any man except his father dealing with his mom feels wrong. I'm not saying you can't re-marry or get married for the first time. What I am saying is you need to think and pray very carefully about having another male around your son. There is never a good reason for you to try out a bunch of guys around your son that have no chance of being "the one". Now I'm going to share something about my mom to show you how her life influenced me. It is *not* intended to dishonor her.

From the time I was eight until I was sixteen, my mom dated a man who was a very nice guy. He was in the military and seemed to know a lot about many different things. He was fun to be around and my sister and I really grew to care for him. He was a photographer with a bunch of equipment, including all the backdrops, lights, cameras, and everything to take pictures. He always had a nice car, nice house, and plenty of money or so we thought. He took us out to eat often and even on vacations. We were kind of like a family. So why didn't he marry my mother and we all live happily ever after?

Well there was this *one* little detail that got in the way. He was already married, with kids. Now mind you, they never talked about this, neither my mom nor her "boyfriend". However, I'll never forget the night I first came to know his wife. We had all gone to bed for the night. My mother and her "boyfriend" were in her room and my sister and I were in our rooms. I was drifting off to sleep when all of a sudden I was jolted wide-awake by the sound of someone banging on the front door. Needless to say, everyone else woke up too. The banging continued and then I heard this woman screaming, "I know you're in there! Come out here! Come out! I know you're in there! Come out and be a man!" This went on for quite some time.

I sat up straight, frozen in my bed, scared to make a noise. It was like I was as guilty as my mom. It got even scarier when this woman started trying to pry the door open. My sister and I gathered in my mother's room.

"Why is this woman going crazy?" my sister and I whispered. My mother's "boyfriend" told us to ignore it, promising that she would go away soon. Well, eventually she did leave, but that experience left an indelible mark on my life. I had already met the three kids from his first marriage, and knew he had two other children with the door-banging lady. But hearing a woman screaming outside my house in the middle of the night made it so clear that what my mother and "her boyfriend" were doing was *wrong*. What I couldn't understand as a kid became really clear as I got older. That woman wasn't crazy, she only wanted what was hers. My mom, a woman who had gone through all the pain and suffering of a broken marriage was breaking up another marriage. Now, knowing my mother, this wasn't her intent, but it was a price that she was willing to pay to soothe her loneliness.

Her loneliness was aiding in the breakup of another woman's marriage. By bringing another woman's husband into our house, she showed my sister and me that marriage vows meant nothing. She made us her accomplices, and we subconsciously carried her guilt for years. She was mis-educating us with her life. She was telling us, silently but clearly, that we were not good enough to have anything of our own. Our best bet was to steal all we could from someone else. *She taught us through what she was doing not what she was saying.* Remember your son will learn far more from what you "do" than he will from what you "say."

Now it's easy to hear that story and criticize my mom. Maybe you've never been with a married man. I can promise you that giving your body to a man who won't marry you or whom you don't want to marry, sends pretty much the same message.

Maybe you don't even date, but you harbor bitterness and rage in your heart. All of these things inside you will poison your son just as if you were putting bug spray in his oatmeal every morning. You have to take a good long look in the mirror and confront the evil influences in yourself, if you want to influence your son for good.

FIVE
What Right Looks Like

A few years ago, while attending a leadership conference in Atlanta, I had the privilege of hearing a lecture by Brigadier General Leo A. Brooks Jr., commandant of the U.S. Corps of Cadets at West Point, the second black man ever to hold this prestigious position. General Brooks shared a story with us of how his cadets were struggling to pass a particular physical abilities test. This was a huge problem because this test was required for graduation. Failing this test was such a widespread problem that West Point officials contemplated lowering the test standards.

General Brooks refused to allow lowering of the standards. His reasoning was that if he had to pass this same test when he was a cadet, there was no reason these cadets couldn't do it. In order to prove that point, he subjected himself to taking the same test again. At twice the age of his cadets, he not only survived the grueling physical trial, but also exceeded the requirements for people half his age. He told us he had to show those students *what right looks like*."

We live in a generation when crowds of "experts" are telling us the way to fix problems is to lower standards or put your son on medicine to help him "slow down and pay attention". They will tell you that you can't expect certain things from your son because he doesn't have a dad or because you don't have a certain amount of money.

By now, I hope you realize that I am NOT saying for one minute that it is easy to be a boy growing up without a dad. It is one of the hardest things I've ever had to do. But if you let your son use this fact as an excuse to be irresponsible or underachieve, you are only harming him more.

At the end of the day, your son will grow up to live in the real world where he'll have to compete against the same standard as everyone else. The longer you allow him to be evaluated against lower standards, the more you are crippling him. Your son may have to work harder at some things than other kids who have both parents in the house and that will not seem fair for him. However, as the old folks used to say, "life ain't fair". If he has to work harder at something, then he has to work harder. Your job is to encourage him through that process. You don't have the power to make everything fair for him, but you do have the power to help him overcome the obstacles he faces.

I've spent a lot of time telling you my story. Hopefully, I've opened your eyes to a perspective that you've not considered before-a boys perspective on life. I have asked a lot of invasive questions and posted many warnings for you. Now, finally! I want to talk to you about what right looks like.

Love and Law

You must understand that as quiet as it's kept, children crave both love and law [some refer to it as discipline]. They also need nurture, affection, and consistent boundaries around their behavior. When they have all of one, none, or little of the other, it disrupts their world. It's like a balanced diet. No one wants to live on salad alone, but a kid that gets only meat will not be in good shape either. You need to *avoid the two extremes of permissiveness and legalism.*

A disobedient child who gets coddled when he should be receiving truthful words will have no tolerance for correction later in life. You may think you are "going easy on him" because of the harsh realities of his life. *However, just as often, you are going easy on yourself.* In fact, I want you to consider the fact that sometimes you may not confront or punish him because you are too selfish to take the time required to do it right.

It is always easier to give in to a child rather than withhold something, whether it's extra dessert or more television. *A loving parent sets firm limits* and sticks with them. For example, two cookies after dinner or one hour of TV per day. A coddled child will begin to think that anyone who speaks truth is out to get him. He will blame others for his mistakes and refuse to accept responsibility for his actions. You have seen the brat in the grocery store that has a fit when he is told, "No, you can't have that." This comes from being told, "yes" too many times to his every desire. Don't let your son become that brat.

On the other hand, you cannot make the mistake of being harsh and legalistic. Remember, the rules aren't there to bog you down; they are to help you. You set limits on addictive things like sweets and entertainment so your son will learn to master those urges in his life. *The rule is a means to an end, not an end in itself.* For example, let's say your eight-year-old son is supposed to have his room clean before he can play outside and he forgets to clean it one time. If he normally does it responsibly, there is no need to jump all over him. Just remind him and he should take care of it. On the other hand, if he is constantly forgetting, you need to consider harsher consequences so he can learn a habit that should be very simple for a child his age.

Parents who are too legalistic either provoke their children to rebel or raise them with a need to control other people. Remember, you have to move beyond control to instilling character. That way, your son will control his own behavior and your job will be much easier!

> **HERE'S A THOUGHT:**
>
> *Punishment is about inflicting pain,*
> *for a wrong done.*
> *Discipline is about pain that's inflicted*
> *that will create a desire to change.*

Honesty

Kids need to be dealt with honestly. They are born with a desire to believe the best about their parents and trust them completely. Unfortunately, by the time Kindergarten rolls around, most parents have wasted this trust. So, honesty has to start with you. If you can't be honest with yourself, your son is in trouble.

It's okay to start out inadequate, ignorant and incomplete. However, it's another thing if you choose to remain that way once you discover the truth. I have already mentioned the need to educate yourself as a parent. In addition to that, it's imperative that you take an honest inventory of your own character and integrity. If you lie to yourself about what is going on inside of you, your son will pick up on that. This then becomes a habit for him that sometimes can take quite a while for him to identify and change.

Unfortunately, I have seen countless mothers lose their sons because of their inability to be honest with themselves. This slowly and steadily erodes your authority with your son. As soon as you try to correct him, he will point out your hypocrisy. If you want better for him, you have to demand better from yourself. If you are honest with you, it empowers you to be honest with him. When that happens, it doesn't matter where your starting point was, you can change.

Consistency

Children also need consistency and routine, and yet "chaos" is the ruler of far too many households. Life is confusing enough; you need to do everything you can to make your son's life peaceful and predictable, especially when he is young. Unless you keep him in a consistent routine of proper hygiene, exercise, schoolwork, and limited entertainment, he'll never learn to be responsible for those things on his own. On the other hand, if you instill these things consistently, he is almost guaranteed to carry that consistency into adulthood.

Less Talk More Consequences

We are still talking about what right looks like and I haven't held back on you so far. I am going to say this as clearly and honestly as I can: *Most women talk way too much.* Most women talk more than men are able to listen, and you and your son are probably no exception.

Remember, when you are dealing with a boy, his language is "consequences" not lectures. If you want your message to really sink in, *use exactly the number of words you need to make your point one time, and then force your son to endure consequences for his actions.*

I remember times I should have had to endure painful loss for very bad choices that I made, but instead, my mother would talk and talk and talk. While she was talking herself blue in the face, I was completely tuning her out. Your son, like almost every male on earth, has a limited capacity for words. Yelling at him to look at you when you are talking will not do anything to make him hear what you're saying. Most of the time, if you're honest with yourself, the lecture is just to vent your own emotions. And while that may be understandable, it is *not* an effective way to raise a child. *Deal with your own emotions first* and then deal with him. Talk to him calmly and firmly and then make him *feel* a loss.

At the end of the day, everyone makes mistakes. People who let their lives be defined by mistakes are the people who refuse to acknowledge the cause and effect of their actions. You want to teach your son that bad choices create a bad life; this means forcing him to feel some of those bad effects. For example, if you catch your son stealing, you have some options: (1) you could lecture him for an hour, or (2) force him to repay five times what he stole? Use common sense to make the punishment fit the crime and apply it without fail. As a parent, I later learned how true this was. My Momma's Boy tendencies often would show themselves in my son. I remember explaining to him the importance of bringing home "everything" he needed to study. When I would ask, "how are you going to do your home work without your text books?" He'd have that crazy distant look in his eyes that all kids have when they don't have an answer. So instead of imposing consequences appropriate for an 8th grader, the Momma's Boy in me would just "fuss" and "talk" to him until I was "blue in the face". Well that went on a few times until it dawned on me that my words where not phasing him in the least bit. So after talking to a close friend about it, he helped me understand that I was "talking too much" and "not doing anything". He would often say "Glenn you have to dish out consequences" and "they have to be consistent. Consistent as a "Hot Iron" he'd say, "everyone knows that if there is one thing you can count on from touching a hot iron, is that it'll burn you EVERY time". Well I decided that the next time he didn't bring everything home and used the old "I forgot and left it in my locker" excuse, I decided that he didn't need a locker.

So I took his locker privileges and made him bring every book for every class home every day for the rest of the quarter. Well, that cured that excuse. Sound extreme? Maybe for you, but what I learned through that experience is that my job is to create an environment for my son to learn that his decisions would bring consequences. If you don't do that you may find the police doing your job for you a few years down the road.

HERE'S A THOUGHT:

Your son wants to comply with you,

he just can't hear you.

Learn his language.

Family Identity

Seventy percent of Black babies in the United States are born out of wedlock. As a result, many of these children may never know the true love of a father. Whatever your circumstance, you are not alone. You can look at your situation from the perspective of how hard it is for you, and, as I've already said, you are right. It is hard for any woman to try to do what you're doing.

Again, my goal for this book has been to help you see that it is also hard for your son. He's already missing his father;

he can't lose you too. You are his only source of family. What will happen to him if you are always exhausted, depressed, or distracted?

Even the mothers who have to work two jobs can give their children a sense of family life. We all know that kids feel peer pressure because of a need to "belong" to something. The family is the first place they should understand how to belong. The less they feel like they belong to a family, the more they'll look to friends and people outside the home to satisfy that need. Momma's Boys are sons who are not secure in their relationships, especially within the family. They tend to be very insecure, hence the need to manipulate and control.

I understand that your time and money are limited, but I want you to carefully think about how you use what you *do* have. Establish special times just for your son that you can both look forward to. Libraries, parks and even some museums are free, as well as many church-sponsored programs.

Do not get weighted down with what you can't do; focus on what you can do. Make the time you do have with him count. At the end of the day what he'll remember is that his mom was "consistently adequate", not perfect but functional. He'll grow up with a solid foundation that can withstand pressure. He will be a wisdom seeker and not a prideful jerk. He will love and care deeply and be able to consider the needs of others. He will have a firm sense of who he is and who he isn't. He will make mistakes as we all do, but he'll be able to stand and confront himself on what would've been a better way to handle that situation and have the courage and discipline to implement the "lesson's learned" the next time around. He won't be a blamer but an accepter of responsibility. He will also be able to teach others by example, not just words. He most assuredly will not become a Momma's Boy but he'll become a highly functional male man, a man fit to be sent out into the world and to make a huge difference in the lives of others. He will make himself proud, and you'll reap some of those benefits also.

CONCLUSION

So now you know part of my story as a Momma's Boy. My hope is that by sharing my pain and my failures, I can open your eyes to some of the dangers lurking down the road for your son, if not handled properly. My own experiences with abuse, sexual addiction, and a failed marriage occurred before the advent of Internet pornography and other new inventions designed to destroy young boys. So in many ways, you have more to fight against than my mom did. I realize that a lot of what I've shared may sound harsh or discouraging, but I'm on a mission to save your son from becoming a Momma's Boy. We must start preparing our sons to navigate the real world and we can't do that if we're not willing to face reality. How can you protect your kids from something that you don't even know is out there? How can you guide your son through a minefield that you won't even admit exists? So much of your son's survival and success depends on your willingness to face the truth.

Remember, it doesn't matter where you start. It only matters that you start where you are. When you decide to "Do the Work", change is not only possible but highly probable. If you focus only on your needs and your problems, you force your son to raise himself and you gamble that some other adult will pick up the slack and help him along. That could happen, but more often than not, others will use your son and throw him away when they're done.

On the other hand, if you are willing to give everything you've got, and then some, you can help him become the man his father never was. You will help him take the journey to becoming a real man, not a Momma's Boy.

ACKNOWLEDGMENTS

Deron and Jill Cloud for your unfailing support
and encouragement. I thank God for your
example of leadership, love, and friendship.

The Soul Factory Theatre Church for giving me
a place to belong, grow, and serve God's
people.

Julia Nelson for helping me to make sense of
my thoughts by putting them in writing.

My mother, Patricia J. Palmore for not giving
up on me and for showing me by example how
not to quit!

My father, Glenn P Brooks, Sr. for being
honest with me when I needed you to be and
being available for me to really share.

Deatra D. Mason for forgiving me for the Hell
I put you through and allowing me to help raise
our son.

Sheri Brooks for a chance to demonstrate to
the world through our marriage that a man can
change.

To those counselors, men, women, friends,
family, some professionals, and some not, that
spoke into my life and showed me how to
process what I experienced growing up. I'll be
forever grateful!

Suggested Reading List for Raising Boys

Mothers and Sons
By: Jean Lush

Running the Rapids:
Your Teen Survive the Turbulent Waters of
Adolescence
By: Kevin Leman

Making Children Mind Without Losing Yours
By: Kevin Leman

Bringing up Boys
By: James Dobson

Countering the Conspiracy to Destroy Black
Boys,
Volumes. 1-4
By: Jawanza Kunjufu

The Minds of Boys:
Saving Our Sons From Falling Behind in
School and Life
By: Michael Gurian and Kathy Stevens

About the Author: Glenn P Brooks, Jr.

Born in South Baltimore Maryland to young parents in 1966, Glenn was raised by a single mother after his parents divorced. Although he experienced a great deal of trauma in his life as a child, Glenn always seemed to have a magnetic personality that made it very easy to capture the attention of others. This quality would ultimately serve to be one of his greatest assets and liabilities.

After High School he joined the Army and served as a Combat Engineer, this experience served as his introduction to the world of leadership. During his military service, Glenn began serving the youth of his local church and there found one of his many passions, to make a difference in the lives of children.

After his military service tour, he went into the broadcasting industry where he continued to grow as a leader, working as an intern, on-air announcer, and Program Director. He later became one of the youngest Station Managers of the top ranked Gospel radio station in the Washington DC radio market.

Today he serves as the Campus Pastor for the Soul Factory Theatre Church-Atlanta, where Deron Cloud is Lead Pastor. Inspiring, motivating, teaching, training and ultimately leading others to understand, that it's not where a man starts that matters, it's where he finishes that counts.

Made in the USA
Columbia, SC
16 January 2019